Mates for Life

Devoted couples
from the
animal kingdom

Mates for Life

AMMONITE
PRESS

First Published 2010 by
Ammonite Press
an imprint of AE Publications Ltd,
166 High Street, Lewes, East Sussex, BN7 1XU

Text © AE Publications Ltd
Images © www.photolibrary.com
© Copyright in the Work AE Publications Ltd

ISBN: 978-1-907708-02-2

British Cataloguing in Publication Data. A catalogue record of this
book is available from the British Library.

Author: George Lewis
Editor: Ian Penberthy
Managing Editor: Richard Wiles
Design: Adam Carter

Font: La Gioconda
Colour reproduction by GMC Reprographics
Printed and bound in China by Hing Yip Printing Co. Ltd

Page 2: Wolf mates make a howling
success of life together.
Page 96: Parting is sweet sorrow, but
emperor penguins faithfully seek
out their mate each year on the icy
wastes of Antarctica.

CONTENTS

INTRODUCTION

When you hear people described as 'animals' you know the term is not being used as a compliment. The assumption is that, while humans may sometimes fall from grace, they are at least capable of behaving morally, whereas in the animal kingdom it is every creature for itself. But while humans claim that sexual fidelity is one of the qualities that distinguishes them from and raises them above the beasts, the fact remains that some animals strike up exclusive relationships that they maintain until death doth them part.

Although some species do mate for life, things are not always as they once appeared. DNA analysis has revealed that bottlenose dolphins, which for thousands of years were regarded as almost human in their capacity for love, are in fact sexually rapacious and tirelessly promiscuous. On the other hand, the good reputation of their cousins, the river dolphins of Asia and South America, remains untarnished. It's tempting to question the motivation of those that do mate for life.

Some species settle down with the only partner they can find, and stay together for want of other opportunities. Snow leopard pairs live in such isolation that the only other members of their species they see are their own cubs. Other couples sequester themselves and fight off sexual adventurers – white rhinos are a case in point. Others stay together for the sake of their offspring – if harlequin frog parents did not work as a team their tadpoles would not reach maturity.

A few have no choice – Canada geese can't escape the responsibilities of parenthood because as soon as the female lays her eggs, both adults lose the ability to fly.

So perhaps the original assumption was correct – animals behave like animals. But the behaviours of many don't look too different from human relationships: several species solicitously provide food for their partners and offspring; marine otter pairs have public fights, but still they stick together. Science cannot determine whether animals are capable of true love, but given the number of similarities between human behaviour and the lifestyles of the mates for life featured here, it would be a brave and foolish person who discounted the possibility that they're more like us than we might care to admit.

GIBBON

Animals that sing together stay together. Deep in the forests of southeast Asia, gibbons mate after an elaborate courtship involving a musical duet in which the female takes the lead vocals and the male joins in with a simpler, but louder and deeper counterpoint. Having hit the right notes, they pair off and the mother gives birth about seven months later to a single baby; the parents then work as a team to rear their pride and joy for the next seven years, by which time it is old enough to fend – and sing – for itself.

BALD EAGLE

After the male bald eagle mates with the rather larger female, the couple sticks together forever – and forever could be as long as thirty years. In their nests, built in tall trees or on rocky outcrops, the birds share parental duties, taking it in turns to sit on the eggs and, after hatching, to provide food for the whole family. The national symbol of the United States, these eagles aren't really bald – the white feathers on their heads just make them look as if they are. They're correctly known as sea eagles, but in addition to fish they may bring home small birds and mammals, snakes, turtles and crabs to delight the taste buds of their offspring.

HARLEQUIN FROG

The key to successful long-term relationships is often elusive, but for the harlequin frog fidelity to one's chosen partner, and the male's active involvement in rearing the young, is imperative to the actual survival of this species of South American amphibian. The father ferries the young to the water straight after hatching while the mother recovers. He then keeps a protuberant eye on them: if they are hungry, he summons the mother to deposit non-fertile eggs in the pool for them to eat. In the absence of either parent, the tadpoles would die.

WOLF

Wolves have family values to which humans can only aspire. Living in packs of six to twenty, composed of one pair of adults and their offspring, they all stay together until – and sometimes even after – the cubs grow up and start their own families. Forget the propaganda, wolves are neither big nor bad: most are smaller than great danes. The wolf's kingdom is a hierarchy: parents run the show, and give short shrift to impudent cubs, communicating their feelings with a wide range of facial expressions, body language, growls, yelps and snarls. Rebellious youths are presented with a stark choice from their parents: shape up or ship out.

BARN OWL

The adult male barn owl, having made a home in an existing cavity or makeshift nest, entices a female to move in with him in a courtship ritual that involves a beguiling shrill whistle. Having formed a pair, the she-owl lays between three and a dozen eggs at a time; she then tends those that hatch for five to six weeks while father devotes himself to providing food for the whole family. These distinctive carnivores are oddly vulnerable to predators and, although barn owls may survive for more than twenty years in captivity, in the wild they seldom live long enough to reproduce.

22 Mates for Life

BEAVER

Beaver pairs remain faithful from first mating until parted by death, which may be after some twenty-four years. In the rivers, lakes and ponds of northern North America, Europe and Asia, these family-oriented creatures form close-knit colonies in which they co-operate to create lodges – calm-water habitats – by building dams from branches gnawed off trees and bushes, and rocks that they have pushed, dragged or carried into position. They produce annually a litter of up to nine young, known as kits, and both male and female adults work hard to raise them in the first year of life. Lodges typically comprise two adults, the new arrivals and the yearlings from the previous litter.

ROBIN

As parents, teamwork is all for the robin redbreast: they build their nest together out of leaves and moss, then line it with feathers before immediately starting a family. With a life expectancy of just over one year, there's no time for a long courtship. The little birds are widely distributed throughout Europe, western Asia, and parts of North Africa. The northernmost birds of the species are migratory, but the southern ones stay put, seemingly content with their environment year-round. During the female's 14-day confinement while incubating the eggs (normally six in number), the male brings home her food (mainly insects). A fortnight after hatching, the new arrivals fly off, leaving the adult pair to start immediately on a second brood.

DIK-DIK

Home sweet home for monogamous pairs of the world's smallest antelope is a territory marked out with dung and urine. The petite dik-dik of the East African bush, standing no taller than 18 inches (45 cm), can do little to defend its home, although when threatened by another dik-dik both male and female emit the cry from which their name derives. This warns the intruder that they are a couple. Females produce a single foal, which leaves as a yearling to seek a mate and a plot of land of its own. But living space is scarce and young dik-diks may have to wait for the death of an older animal before they can set up home.

WOLF EEL

The fearsome looking wolf eel forms pairs at the age of about four, which stay together for three years before laying eggs in a submarine nest, which is then guarded by both parents in turn while the other looks for food (mainly crabs, clams and mussels). Newborns eat plankton before graduating to the adult diet. They swim around freely until they take their turn to settle down with a partner. Wolf eels are not true eels but fish. Neither are they as aggressive as they look, although they have been known to snap at scuba divers in their main habitat, the Pacific coastal waters between Alaska and California.

ANDEAN CONDOR

In a perfect world, the Andean condor would breed in alternate years. In the real one, their single egg often fails to produce a fledgling. One of the main causes of death is falls from the high rocky outcrops on which they settle: condors do not build nests. When they suffer a loss, the male and female are united in grief and try again together 12 months later. These birds have a much better public image than their close relatives, the vultures, because while the latter appear scrawny and scarcely airworthy, the South American giants look as robust as light aircraft soaring high on white-tipped wings.

SWAN

Swan pairs form monogamous bonds that can last for life, and even after their 'ugly duckling' offspring have metamorphosed into mature birds, the young often choose to stick around their parents for the rest of their lives. It's a myth that swans sing only when they die. They are among the chattiest of aquatic birds – in spite of their name, even mute swans grunt – until they finish courting. The female (pen) then sits in silence on the eggs (up to six of them), while the only sounds the male (cob) makes are hisses to repel nest botherers. Once hatched, the young (cygnets) are looked after by both parents; pens ferry them on their backs for months even though they can swim within hours of birth.

RAVEN

After a courting ritual that involves breathtaking aerobatics, ravens form monogamous pairs. Such exclusive relationships may be long: they begin when the birds are around a year old, and they may live for more than half a century. Members of the crow family that have lived close to humans for thousands of years, ravens have earned a reputation for resourcefulness and intelligence – although also as symbols of grim foreboding, especially harbingers of death. They nest in tumbledown structures built from thick sticks. The young take around a month to fledge; both parents take active roles in the process.

38 Mates for Life

CHINCHILLA

After mating, the male chinchilla remains with his female partner for the entire gestation period of 111 days, and the cute couple may stay together for the rest of their lives, up to twenty years. In their native habitat of Chile and Peru, chinchilla couples live with others in colonies in rock crevices. Once very common, these Andean creatures were hunted so mercilessly for their dense, silky fur that by the start of the 20th century they faced extinction. They were saved partly by increasing environmental awareness and mainly by the export to the United States in 1927 of thirteen individuals, from which every modern pet chinchilla is descended.

FRENCH ANGELFISH

Although members of this species normally swim around in pairs whether they are spawning or not, the lasting bond between parents is forged by the need to protect their eggs from the numerous predators that maraud their habitat, the shallow coral reefs of the Caribbean and the Gulf of Mexico, and the Atlantic coast of northern South America. Attractive to behold with their golden fin rims on a black background, large (up to 16 inches/40 cm long), fleshy and good to eat, French angelfish are particularly targeted by humans, who catch them to sell on food stalls and for tropical aquaria.

42 Mates for Life

SANDHILL CRANE

At the age of around two years, the instincts of these migratory birds turn to finding a mate and starting a family. After breeding in the spring in North America and Siberia, they flock together to fly south, where the parents introduce their offspring to the charms of the Caribbean winter. In time off from raising their young, mated pairs – which can stick together for a quarter of a century – stand close together and practise unison calling: the female makes one harsh cry and the male responds with two identical sounds. Sandhill crane pairs have been used as surrogate parents for the endangered whooping crane.

VICTORIA CROWNED PIGEON

Like all 250 pigeon species – and indeed the queen for whom it is named – the Victoria crowned pigeon mates for life. After the death of one partner, the survivor rarely takes a new mate and may even appear to mourn, just as the British monarch did for forty years after the death in 1861 of her beloved husband Prince Albert. The female lays a single white egg that is incubated for between two and three weeks; both parents then look after the hatchling for another fortnight. The Victoria crowned pigeon of New Guinea, a big, somewhat heavy bird, is immediately identifiable by the white tips on its crest.

AFRICAN WILD DOG

In a world of promiscuity among the weaker or younger members of an African wild dog pack, the alpha male and female – leaders of the gang – are faithful to each other for life. In the packs of between 10 and 20 individuals, the animals' breeding habits are well established: at the start of the season they suspend their normal wanderings and settle down in a quiet secluded spot – often an abandoned aardvark nest – and await the birth of the pups after a gestation period of 70 days. They remain there until the young are weaned at about 10 weeks and then move on.

RIVER DOLPHIN

While recent studies and DNA tests have done much to discredit the long-held notion that bottlenose dolphin pairs are faithful to each other for life, the reputation for fidelity of their cousins, the river dolphins – four species that inhabit some freshwater estuaries, mainly those of the Ganges and Indus rivers in Asia, but also some in South America – remains untarnished (although mainly for lack of evidence). While the reasons for their devotion remain unknown, some naturalists have speculated that it is simply because they live in smaller groups than the bottlenoses and therefore have less opportunity to fool around.

AMERICAN BLACK VULTURE

After an elaborate courtship ritual in which competing males strut with heads bobbing and partially opened wings around the desired female, these scavengers mate for life. They may also show off their aerobatic prowess, chasing each other through the air while the females look on from terra firma. Widely distributed throughout the Americas, the vultures, after pairing off, breed between January and March in the northern hemisphere and in September–October to the south of the equator. They lay their eggs – up to three in a clutch – in ground nests. Hatchlings are fed by both parents, who take it in turns to regurgitate food for them.

ALBATROSS

Despite spending up to 10 years of their lives at sea, albatrosses find time to forge lifelong relationships with the opposite sex and are thought to be one of the few creatures that die of old age. The albatross has no natural enemies apart from humans – Coleridge's Ancient Mariner is the most famous slayer of this gigantic bird. In the breeding season, albatross males slap their beaks against each other and both sexes make wing-spreading displays. The female lays a single egg and it is almost a year before a chick can fend for itself. Meanwhile the adults form ties that endure even after the young has flown: empty-nest syndrome binds the parents forever.

SEA OTTER

Many species of sea otter form lifelong bonds with a single partner, although, as with their human counterparts, the course of an otter's true love does not always run smooth: fights have been observed on seaside rocks between long-established pairs. Mysterious mammals that inhabit rocky shorelines along the southwest coast of South America, they mate in midsummer (December–January) and the females give birth around 10 weeks later to between two and five pups. The offspring remain with the parents for 10 months until they have learned to hunt for the crabs and shrimps, molluscs and small fish that sustain them.

EMPEROR PENGUIN

The largest penguin species is famous for fidelity, returning to the same mate annually. Emperor pairs form tight units – they have to, because the threats to their reproduction are immense. Part of their problem is that they do not build nests; the male incubates their single egg for nine weeks on his flippers. While he survives on fat reserves, the female fishes in the sea, which may be up to 100 miles (160 km) from the Antarctica colony. Mother and father then take turns to guard their hatchling from predatory birds while the other searches for food. It is six months before the baby can fend for itself.

SILVER-BACKED JACKAL

After mating, many silver-backed jackals live together in pairs, within packs, and remain faithful to each other for life, although this is not achieved without some cost: they often have to fight off lothario jackals that approach the female with bad intentions. Also known as the black-backed jackal, this species lives in two distinct areas of Africa: the southern tip between Botswana and the Cape, and along the central eastern coast. They are nocturnal animals that celebrate nightfall by emitting blood-curdling howls. Although they may hunt antelope or sheep, they subsist mainly on the leftovers from lion kills.

OSPREY

Ospreys form lifelong pairs and return annually to the same breeding grounds. Their offspring may take over the nests in which they themselves were reared. Female birds lay up to four eggs that hatch five weeks later; chicks are nurtured by both parents until they are fledged after about two months. This magnificent sea hawk is widely distributed throughout the world, but in the late 19th century its eggs became so popular with collectors that by 1910 it had been exterminated in the British Isles. Its reintroduction to Scotland in the 1950s was an emblematic triumph for the nascent conservation movement.

SEAHORSE

Some people think that men get off lightly in the reproductive process, but objectors to that assertion would have to admit that the involvement of even the newest new man bears no comparison with the role of male sea horses. After elaborate courtship rituals, the female deposits her eggs in a pouch in the male's tail. As the foetuses mature, the bodily fluids inside the sac are gradually replaced by salt water. Once the change is complete, the babies are expelled into the sea and left to fend for themselves, leaving the parents to start a new family immediately.

GUINEA FOWL

These colourful members of the pheasant family choose lifelong mates and soon set about raising a family. The females lay up to a dozen eggs that require thirty days' incubation. The chicks are covered in fluffy down, and their parents accompany them everywhere until they are fully fledged. Originally from eastern Africa, guinea fowl have been introduced by humans to other parts of the world, most successfully in the West Indies. They make raucous cawing noises when disturbed, and are sometimes used to guard cattle and other livestock. They normally sleep in trees, but nest on the ground.

SNOW LEOPARD

Snow leopards mate towards the end of winter, the females giving birth to between two and four cubs after a gestation period of around 13 weeks. The parents remain together for life. While it is tempting to anthropomorphise this behaviour as devotion, it's likely that the cats' reclusive nature makes it hard for either partner to find another mate. This endangered species lives in the mountains of central Asia and the Indian subcontinent. It spends the winter months at heights of around 18,000 feet (5,500 m), then moves in summer to even higher ground to avoid the heat.

TURTLE DOVE

Synonymous in Western culture with eternal love, this pretty member of the pigeon family is mentioned in the Bible (The Song of Solomon) and in Shakespeare. Two of them are among the true love's gifts to the singer in 'The Twelve Days of Christmas'. The turtle dove's mating ritual involves a high, circling flight in which the birds make whip-cracking noises by flicking their wings downwards. The turtle dove is named for its spring call – a deep, purring 'turr-turr' – and has no link to the shelled reptile. A migratory species, it spends its summers in Europe and winters in North Africa.

EMU

The flightless Australian emu – after the ostrich, the world's second largest bird – chooses its partner in December and January, at the height of the antipodean summer, then mates in the coldest winter months (May and June). The male plays a major pre-natal role, building a ground nest in a naturally occurring hollow and then incubating the female's aquamarine eggs (between seven and ten per clutch) throughout their 60-day term. During this period, he undergoes significant hormonal changes that rob him of his appetite: he survives on accumulated body fat.

WHITE RHINOCEROUS

Romance knows no bounds in the animal kingdom. When he takes a mate, the dominant adult bull rhinocerous brings her into the sanctum of the territory he has marked, not with red roses, but with dung and urine, and maintains the exclusive right to her affections by fighting off any trespassers. Although some submissive members of this African species may live in herds of between 10 and 14 individuals, dominant adult bulls are solitary. His time is taken up patrolling his territory regularly and fiercely defending his land claim against all intruders, especially fellow males of the same species. In the mid-20th century, the white rhino was one of the world's most endangered animals, but since then careful preservation has enabled its numbers to recover to sustainable levels.

CANADA GOOSE

As soon as they reach maturity after a year, Canada geese set about finding a mate and, once the choice has been made, they remain as a couple for the rest of their lives. After the female has laid her eggs – between three and eight per clutch – an amazing change comes over both parents: they lose their flight feathers and are grounded. Thus they have no distractions from their prime task, to protect the nest. Four weeks later, when the goslings are hatched, the adults regain their ability to fly and, once the youngsters have fledged at between six and nine weeks, lead their offspring in skeins across the sky.

FLAMINGO

The same pair of adult flamingoes may mate again and again, and set about building a nest from wet mud clay that they pile up until it stands a couple of inches above the surface of their lagoon, where they congregate in great flocks along the shores of East Africa. The female lays one or two eggs, which are tended by both parents during the incubation period of around four weeks. The chicks first venture out two or three days after hatching, but are still fed for some months on plankton that has been regurgitated by their parents. When they take to the air, a group formation of flamingoes may darken the sky.

MAGPIE

Adult magpies form lifelong partnerships that begin with the construction of large and highly robust round nests of twigs cemented with mud. They then settle down to produce several sets of chicks, between five and eight per clutch. The parents take a firm line with their young, forbidding them to caw – this is understandable in view of the fact that each bird is capable of producing 127 decibels; louder than a pneumatic drill. These noisy omnivores of the crow family are commonplace in the farmlands and woods of Britain, mainland Europe, Asia, North Africa and western North America.

AMMONITE
PRESS

Contact us for a complete catalogue or visit our website:
Ammonite Press, 166 High Street, Lewes, East Sussex, BN7 1XU, United Kingdom
Tel: +44 (0)1273 488006 Fax: +44 (0)1273 472418
www.ammonitepress.com